Program Evaluation:

A Step-by-Step Guide

(Revised Edition)

Nancy F. Barrett EdD

Sunnycrest Press

Springfield, IL

www.sunnycrestpress.com

ISBN: 978-0-9883948-9-6

Library of Congress Control Number: 2015911223

This book is dedicated to the hard-working and conscientious program managers, directors, and unit leaders who never in a million years thought their jobs would involve "Evaluation."

Table of Contents

Introduction

As a busy professional, you may be asked to reduce programs, cut budgets, or change staffing patterns. How can you make good recommendations? By implementing a comprehensive evaluation!

Program Evaluation: A Step-By Step Guide (Revised Edition) will teach you how to design and implement a thorough evaluation. By "demystifying" the evaluation process, you will have the knowledge, skills and confidence to help you make these difficult decisions.

Part 1 will give you just enough theory to understand the principles of evaluation. This section will:

- Define evaluation
- Describe the three main evaluation purposes and
- Identify different types of evaluations

Part 2 will provide you with a practical road map for conducting your own evaluation. Here you will learn how to:

- Write good questions
- Collect and analyze data and
- Report the results

Part 3 goes a beyond the basics of evaluation and introduces you to:

- Delphi Interview techniques
- Critical Incident reporting and
- Root Cause Analysis

The Appendices provide practical information about evaluation including:

- An evaluation template
- Reporting guidelines and
- Evaluation resources

Throughout the process, we will refer to a scenario so you will have an example to refer to along the way.

Please note that the focus of this book is on evaluating *programs* and not individuals. If you are interested in measuring employee performance, Kirkpatrick's *Levels of Learning Model* is a good place to start. I have included information about this method in Appendix 1.

We will now get started with basic terms and concepts important in understanding the program evaluation process.

Part 1.

Evaluation Terms and Concepts

"The pure and simple truth is rarely pure and never simple."

-Oscar Wilde

Definition

Just what is an evaluation? Here is a simple working definition:

Program evaluation is the determination of the value or worth of a product, process or program.

Implicit in this definition is that SOMEONE makes a value judgment about the activity in question.

That "someone" is the evaluator!

To be good at it, the evaluator needs a combination of knowledge of evaluation methods, discretion, positivity and keen observational skills.

Let's think about why we evaluate in the first place.

Evaluation Purposes

There are three reasons to do a program evaluation:

1 To identify new programs (Needs Assessment)

2 To change an existing programs (Improvement)

3 To describe outcomes in a completed program (Justification).

Table 1 summarizes these three evaluation purposes and describes their potential uses.

Table 1. Evaluation Types, Purposes and Uses		
Type	**Purpose**	**Possible Uses**
Needs Assessment	Identify new programs	Reach new audiences; increase revenue
Improvement	Make adjustments	Increase efficiency
Justification	Document goal attainment	Reporting to funding agencies

The **needs assessment** seeks to expand services. This can occur either by building on existing strengths and abilities or by identifying unmet needs.

An **improvement** evaluation focuses on an existing program and seeks ways to make it better.

A **justification** evaluation identifies ways that the program or activity has met its stated goals. This function is particularly important when reporting results to funding agencies.

Whatever the purpose of the evaluation, one good way to learn about the process is to follow a scenario as you learn. Read through this simulated case and think about how an evaluation might be used. We will refer back to it many times as we proceed through our discussion of evaluation so keep this situation in mind.

Evaluation Scenario:

You work for Milgram Book Publishing Company.
Because of the changes in the industry and compe-
tition from electronic book publishers, your com-
pany has recently merged with another publisher,
Quantum Books. Your new company is now called
Omega Publishers.

It has been six months since the merger occurred. There
have been some lay-offs, the EPUB section is
expanding and new products are being considered.
Although Omega Publishing still has to work out
some of the details, the new CEO wants to know
how things are going and she has asked you to help.

We are learning that evaluations can be used to identify new programs, improve existing programs or document that you have achieved specific goals.

Another way to think about these different evaluation purposes is to consider activities oriented in time, as Arden Groteleuschen[1] did. This approach may help you better understand these three evaluation purposes.

Table 2 builds on the evaluation purposes outlined earlier in Table 1. Now we add a fourth element: Time.

Look first at Needs Assessment. We see it is *future-oriented* because you want to develop new programs. If you need to improve an existing program, you will be focused on the *present*. And if you want to determine if you have met your goals, you will be looking at *past* achievements.

It is not uncommon to have some combination of past, present and future orientations especially if you are evaluating a complex project or activity as presented in our scenario.

Table 2. **Temporal Orientation of Evaluation**			
Type	**Purpose**	**Possible Uses**	**Time**
Needs Assessment	Identify new programs	Reach new audiences; increase revenue	Future
Improvement	Make adjustments	Increase efficiency	Present
Justification	Document goal attainment	Reporting to funding agencies	Past

We will explore this more in Part 2, but for now, just keep this in mind as we move on to different types of evaluations.

Types of Evaluation

Evaluations can be described in different ways: **who** does the evaluation; **how** it is organized; and the **type of data** that is collected. This section will address each of these evaluation types, starting with who designs and implements the study.

Whether the evaluation is best conducted by someone from within the organization (an internal evaluation) or by an outside consultant (external evaluation) is the very first consideration in structuring the evaluation. Both types of evaluations can provide useful information. Both have strengths and both have weaknesses.

Internal Evaluation

An *internal evaluation* is an assessment of a program, product or service directed by an employee of the organization.

There are three major strengths associated with this approach:

1. The evaluator is familiar with the program and problems.
2. The evaluator may have better/easier access to the data sources.
3. An internal evaluation may better identify new programs or improve existing ones.

However, internal evaluations also have some weaknesses:

1. The evaluator may have a vested interest in the outcomes so he or she may bring biases.[2]
2. He or she may be reluctant to raise sensitive issues.
3. He or she may not have the expertise needed to conduct a thorough evaluation.

External Evaluation

An external evaluation is an assessment of a program, product or service completed by someone from outside the organization.

This approach has strengths which include:

1. Potentially higher objectivity.

2. Possibly more freedom to point out issues and problems.

3. Expertise and experience to conduct a comprehensive evaluation.

An external evaluation may better identify new programs or document outcome attainment, especially for externally funded programs and grants.

Potential weaknesses of an external evaluation include:

1. Unfamiliarity of the evaluator with the organization.

2. More difficulty accessing data.

3. Increased direct costs (although the internal evaluation will still have costs in terms of staff time.)

 Tip 1. *External evaluations may be required for grant-funded projects or programs.*

Table 3 summarizes and compares these two evaluation types.

Table 3. Comparison of Internal and External Evaluations		
	Internal Evaluations	**External Evaluations**
Purpose	Program Improvement Needs Assessment.	Outcome Attainment Needs Assessment.
Expertise	Resides in the organization.	Resides with the expert.
Greatest Strength	More access to data and resources. Knows program and setting.	More experience with evaluation. More objective in assessing outcomes.
Greatest Weakness	Expertise and objectivity.	Access to internal data and resources. Unfamiliar with program.

Tip 2. *Consider a "hybrid" approach to evaluation. Do those parts that you feel you can do on your own and work with a professional evaluator when you need help.*

Let's revisit our scenario and think about how internal or external evaluations might be used.

Evaluation Scenario:

You work for Milgram Book Publishing Company. Because of the changes in the industry and competition from electronic book publishers, your company has recently merged with another publisher, Quantum Books. Your new company is now called Omega Publishers.

It has been six months since the merger occurred. There have been some lay-offs, the EPUB section is expanding and new products are being considered. Although Omega Publishing still has to work out some of the details, the new CEO wants to know how things are going and she has asked you to help.

Because the evaluation needs to be comprehensive and serve multiple purposes, you could conduct either an internal or external evaluation. In this case, your decision to choose an internal or external evaluator will depend largely on the resources (time and talent) that you have at your disposal. Either an internal or external evaluation could be appropriate. You may even consider a combination of both.

A Note About Smaller Projects

This scenario involves a large, comprehensive project and asks large, comprehensive questions. You will most likely find yourself facing smaller problems and questions on a daily basis. If this is the case, you can use the tools and principles you are learning here to address these more focused issues. In fact, answering less complex question can be a great way to get started with evaluation.

Such projects can:

- Provide a way to break a large evaluation down into manageable "chunks."
- Allow you to address an emergent issue in a timely fashion.
- Provide data to feed into a larger evaluation later on.

Here's an example of a smaller project based on our scenario:

> ### *Small Scale Project*
>
> *You have just found out that there is a quality issue with eBooks. You are getting customer complaints that they are not downloading properly.*

While you are still engaged in the large scale evaluation, this is something that needs immediate attention because you can't have dissatisfied customers!

Using the strategies you are learning, you can solve this problem and get information for the larger report. By doing this, only will you learn more about the technical side of your business but you will also gain experience in the problem-solving process that might be generalized to other aspects of your organization.

Remember that no matter the size or scope of your evaluation project:

- If you are more interested in **improving an existing program**, an internal evaluation may give you better information.
- If you need to **evaluate outcomes**, especially for an outside funder, an external evaluation may not only be optimal but required.
- If you want to **determine future directions** either an internal or external evaluation would be a appropriate choice.

We will now consider other ways to structure the evaluation.

Logic Models

One popular organization strategy is the Logic Model approach. A Logic Model is a planning tool that clarifies and graphically displays what your project intends to do and what it hopes to accomplish. See *National Network of Libraries of Medicine:* http://nnlm. gov/outreach/community/logicmodel.html for a good example.

Logic Models show the interactions of program **Inputs** (resources), **Outputs** (activities), and **Long** and **Short Term Outcomes** (results). Logic Models are often required for government funded grants because of their ability to clearly show the relationships among program elements. See Evaluation Resources (Appendix 4) for more information about Logic Models.

Qualitative or Quantitative Data

Another way to classify and organize evaluations is by the type of data you will collect.

Qualitative data describes the characteristics of a process or activity. Individual evaluators are largely responsible for gathering, organizing, analyzing and reporting the results. Common types of qualitative data include existing documents, direct or indirect observation of activities, focus groups and interviews.

Quantitative data can be counted and statistically analyzed. This type of information is not as dependent on evaluator opinion and is often viewed as more objective and factual. Examples of quantitative data sources include pre-post testing, surveys, randomized controlled trials and cohort studies.

Both types of data are often collected in comprehensive evaluations and both have strengths and limitations. Table 4 provides a summary of these two data sources and compares them in terms of purpose, strengths, weaknesses and use.

Table 4.
Comparison of Qualitative and Quantitative Evaluations

	Qualitative	Quantitative
Purpose	Answers the question "*Why* is this happening?"	Answers the question *What* is happening?"
Major Strength	Describes the **process**	Describes the **outcome**
Major Weakness	Lack of objectivity	Lack of context
Principal Use	Needs assessment, Program improvement	Outcome attainment

"Mixed Methods" Approach

While qualitative and quantitative methods each have their staunch defenders and equally staunch detractors, fortunately for us, the field of education allows us to use all methods. This common-sense, pragmatic mixed methods approach draws data from many different sources. Focusing on the evaluation purpose, this method starts with the evaluation question. You then identify the best data sources to answer those questions. As the name implies, data for the evaluation will come from the best source, whether it is qualitative or quantitative. This is the approach I take in evaluation projects. We will see an example when we look at the sample plan in Part 2.

But before delving into the planning process, it is important to first take a look at the differences between "evaluation" and "research."

Evaluation or Research?

These two terms are sometimes confused and for good reason: Both answer questions. Both employ an organized approach. And both use similar methods. However, there are key differences:

- Evaluations are focused on a specific situation. Research is more global.

- Evaluation seeks to improve or describe a particular program. Research seeks to add to general knowledge.

- Evaluation focuses on the case at hand. Research looks for ways to apply the results to other settings.

In other words, an evaluation focuses on a specific program, product, problem, or process in terms of identifying future needs, improving some aspect of the project or determining whether intended goals have been met. This focus drives the entire evaluation process, making the questions we ask specific to that particular setting.

Compare this to research. Since research by definition is interested in testing or generating theory, the research questions and goals will revolve around that. Plus, it is very important for research results to be able to be used in other settings. Table 5 compares and contrasts evaluation and research in terms of focus, goals, questions and something called generalizability.[3]

	Evaluation	Research
Table 5. Differences Between Evaluation and Research		
Focus	Specific program/ project	Theory
Questions	Specific to the project	General
Goal	Improvement, Needs Assessment or Justification	Increase knowledge
Interest in Generalizability?	No	Yes

Sometimes the distinctions between evaluation and research can get a bit fuzzy and you may find that your evaluation project actually generates a potential research question. If you are interested in showing how well a specific program has worked, you may want to share the results of your study at a professional conference or submit an article to a journal. This is where you need to be a bit careful because to do so may require the approval of your Institutional Review Board (IRB).

Tip 3. *Check with your research department prior to starting an evaluation project if you think there is a chance you might want to share results outside your organization. This is especially true if you want to share any kind of sensitive or protected data.*

Summary

By now, you should have the idea that evaluations can serve multiple purposes and take different forms. They can be used to improve an existing program, identify new activities or justify expenditures of time and money. They are focused around specific questions and these questions are answered using different data collection methods.

Now that you have the basics, you are ready to see how this all works. Part 2 describes the "nuts and bolts" of developing an evaluation plan.

Part 2.

Evaluation "Nuts and Bolts"

> **❝The most serious mistakes are not being made as a result of wrong answers. The truly dangerous thing is asking the wrong question.❞**
> **-Peter Drucker**

To implement an effective evaluation, you need several things: Good questions, a good plan, a way to collect and organize your data and reporting the results. This section will show you how to develop a comprehensive plan starting with good evaluation questions.

What's the Question ???

Writing good evaluation questions is the first step in the evaluation process. The questions focus the entire project and keep you on track. Because evaluations can be extensive and expensive, you only want to engage in high yield activities that will give you information to answer your questions. In other words, you only want to collect information that relates to what you want to know. Conversely, you want to *use all the data you spent so much time collecting.*

Good questions are focused, concise, and measurable. It is best to start out with one or two broad questions and then add specific ones. Let's revisit our scenario.

Evaluation Scenario:

You work for Milgram Book Publishing Company. Because of the changes in the industry and competition from electronic book publishers, your company has recently merged with another publisher, Quantum Books. Your new company is now called Omega Publishers.

It has been six months since the merger occurred. There have been some lay-offs, the EPUB section is expanding and new products are being considered. Although Omega Publishing still has to work out some of the details, the new CEO wants to know how things are going and she has asked you to help.

Now look again at Table 1.

Table 1.
Evaluation Types, Purposes and Uses

Type	Purpose	Possible Uses
Needs Assessment	Identify new programs	Reach new audiences; increase revenue
Improvement	Make adjustments	Increase efficiency
Justification	Document goal attainment	Reporting to funding Agencies

Remember that a **needs assessment** would identify new activities, an **improvement evaluation** would help us see what we might change and a **justification evaluation** would look at whether we have achieved our goals.

Since something like our company merger is a major undertaking, the evaluation will have multiple purposes. You will want to see what is working, find out what else might be needed, and document that you are meeting your goals. This means that your evaluation questions will need to address ALL THREE purposes of evaluation.

Your overall questions might look something like this:

1. How well has the merger gone? (**Justification**)

2. Are there new projects or products that should be developed? (**Needs Assessment**)

3. Are there changes that can be made to the current system? (**Improvement**)

These three questions are very good starting points for your evaluation of the merger. You will need to develop a few more focused questions, but you are well on your way.

What's the Plan???

> **"I know that half of my advertising dollars are wasted . . . I just don't know which half."**
> **Jon Wanamaker**

Taking a little time to think about and develop your plan will save you tons of time later. I have found that keeping these basic elements in mind helps me focus the evaluation and stay on track:

1. Briefly describe the problem.

2. Identify why it is important to address the problem.

3. Do a literature search to see what else has been done in this area. (See Tip 4. below)

4. Identify your goals for the evaluation.

5. Define your evaluation questions.

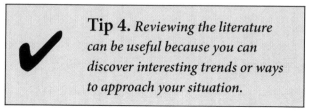

Tip 4. *Reviewing the literature can be useful because you can discover interesting trends or ways to approach your situation.*

Let's see how this might work in our scenario.

1. Briefly describe the problem.

   We want to know how well the merger has gone, if there are additional processes, products or programs needed and if there are ways that current systems could be improved.

2. Identify why it is important to resolve this problem.

   The merger represents a significant financial investment and needs to go well.

3. Do a literature search to see what has been done in this area. (Optional)

   Google Scholar did not reveal recent articles on evaluating mergers. American Society of Training and Development and the American Evaluation Association had some useful articles.

Tip 5. *When doing searches, check with professional associations for reference material. You might also enlist the help of your university or city librarian. They have extensive training that can save you time. Librarians are also usually very willing to help.*

4. Identify what you hope to accomplish by doing the evaluation.

We will develop a comprehensive report of how the merger has affected customers, employees and management, what we might do to improve our process and additional products or programs that might be needed. Note that this mirrors the purposes of evaluation.

5. Evaluation Questions. Identify your three major evaluation questions and then develop **two or three** focused sub-questions for each area. Make sure the questions are specific and relevant! Try to limit the number of questions because you will need to gather data to answer them. Data collection can be time-consuming, so focusing your efforts is important.

Justification: How well has the merger gone?

1. How does the current shipment process compare to the pre-merger system?

2. How satisfied are customers with the new system?

3. How satisfied are staff and managers with the new system?

Needs Assessment: Are there new projects or products that could or should be developed?

1. What new products have you identified via web searches, attending professional conferences, or reading journals?

2. What have customers requested?

3. Are there any barriers to making these changes?

Improvement: Are there changes that can or should be made to the current system?

1. What do staff and managers suggest to improve existing products, service or processes?

2. What suggestions do customers have to improve existing products, service or processes?

3. How might the current shipment system be improved?

By this time, you have identified the problem and why it is important to address this problem. You may have done a lit search (or asked someone else to do this for you) to see how others have handled similar problems. You have a good idea of what you want the evaluation to accomplish. And you have identified the questions that will give you the information that you need.

The next step in the process is to figure out **how** to answer those questions, which means you will need to identify the sources of data you will collect.

Data Sources

> **“First get your facts; then you can distort them at your leisure.”**
> **—Mark Twain**

Mark Twain certainly got the first part right. Gather data!

Here are some useful tips to keep in mind when you are planning to collect data for your evaluation:

General Data Collection Tips

1. Remember to review information that already exists (e.g. user manuals, procedures, correspondence, meeting minutes, program descriptions, and history).

2. Enter your data into a spreadsheet/database and map it to the question or questions it answers.

3. For qualitative data (e.g., comments, interviews) consult with an expert on content analysis to help with proper coding.

4. Consult with a data expert early on to develop good data collection instruments. It can save you time in the long run.

5. ** **Remember: only collect data that will directly answer one of your questions!** While it may be tempting to add more questions to your survey or do more interviews, try to resist the urge to do so and stick to your original plan.

Principal data collection methods for evaluations include surveys, focus groups, interviews, observations, and document reviews. We will look at each of these data types starting with surveys.

Types of Surveys

A survey is a list of questions designed to help you better understand a specific activity or interaction. While there are many different types of surveys, three of the most commonly used in evaluation are forced-choice, open-ended and scaled.

Forced-choice questions require the respondent to select answers from a prescribed list. This type of survey can be very useful when you know a lot about a topic and want to make the survey easier for the respondent to complete. It also helps in the analysis later on, but your primary purpose is ease of use for your respondent. However, even if you think you have listed every possible choice, you should still include an "other" option. This gives the respondent the ability to add information and may even provide new insights you had not considered.

Tip 6. *Unless a survey is required by your employer, "opt out" options are considered best practice and are required for Institutional Review Board (IRB) approval. Check with your Research or Quality Improvement department for guidelines or restrictions.*

Figure 1 provides examples of different types of forced choice questions.

1. What is your gender? (Please choose one.)
   ❒ Male   ❒ Female   ❒ I prefer not to say

2. How long have you been with either Milgram or Quantum? (Please choose one.)

   ❒ Less than one year   ❒ 1-3years

   ❒ 4-6 years   ❒ 7-10 years

   ❒ 11-15 years   ❒ More than15 years

3. What was your primary role in your old company? (Please choose one.)

   ❒ Customer Service   ❒ HR

   ❒ Data entry   ❒ Web Support

   ❒ IT Support   ❒ Management

   ❒ Billing   ❒ I prefer not to say

   ❒ Other (please list.)_____

Figure 1. Examples of forced-choice survey questions.

Note the following in these examples:

1. There are clear instructions.

2. All response options (including the option NOT to respond) are provided.

3. For questions with ranges, (e.g., Question 2) all options are indicated.

4. Question 3 provides space for an additional response.

Open-Ended survey questions require respondents to write or keyboard their answers. Responses can range from one or two word answers to long essays.

Examples are provided in Figure 2.

In Figure 2, Question 1 is very broad and requires a longer response while Question 2 merely requests a list of three items. Both types can provide useful information. You will need to put some thought into it beforehand.

---

1. How has the merger affected you?

2. Please list the three things that you think would make the transition easier for our customers.

1. _____

2. _____

3. _____

Figure 2. Sample open-ended questions.

If you are interested in learning about attitudes or beliefs, *scaled surveys* can do that for you. Scaled surveys include a range of response options that measure attitudes such as agreement, importance, difficulty, frequency, likelihood or quality.

Survey questions can often be asked in different ways. Figure 3 below shows how Question 1 in Figure 2 could be reworded as a scaled item.

In this example, we provided the list of job functions and asked the employees to assess how difficult their post-merger interactions have been with each job category. We have included a scale with the range of options *Very Difficult* to *Very Easy* and have also included a *"No Opinion"* option.

	Very Difficult	Difficult	No Affect	Easy	Very Easy	No Opinion
We are interested in how the merger has affected you. Please rate the difficulty you have had with the merger in each of the following areas. Please select the response that best describes your experience in each area.						
Customer Service	1	2	3	4	5	0
Data Entry	1	2	3	4	5	0
IT Support	1	2	3	4	5	0
Billing	1	2	3	4	5	0
Management	1	2	3	4	5	0
HR	1	2	3	4	5	0
Web Support	1	2	3	4	5	0

Figure 3. Sample scaled survey questions.

Popular scales used to measure attitudes and beliefs include:

Agreement: *Strongly Agree, Agree, Undecided, Disagree, Strongly Disagree*

Importance: *Very Important, Important, Neither Important or Unimportant, Unimportant, Very Unimportant*

Frequency: *Very Frequently, Frequently, Occasionally, Rarely, Very Rarely*

Likelihood: *Almost Always True, Often True, Occasionally True, Usually Not True, Almost Never True*

Quality: *Extremely Poor, Below Average, Average, Above Average, Excellent*

Source: Siegel, D (2010) Likert Scales. University of Connecticut.

Here are some general tips for using scaled surveys that you may find useful:

1. Provide ALL response options including "Don't Know" or "Undecided."

2. Have AT LEAST three response options per item.

3. Make sure the response options are clearly listed at the top of the survey question.

4. Make sure the scaling is consistent (e.g., Strongly Agree, Agree; Neither; Disagree; Strongly Disagree).

5. Try to avoid "Always" and "Never" as response options.

6. Try to have an evenly spaced range of options (e.g., two positive, one neutral, two negative responses).

7. If you want respondents to make a positive or negative choice, leave out the middle or neutral option and choose a four-point scale instead.

8. Use previously tested survey questions and scales when possible.

If you want to learn more about survey research, I have included a list of websites in Appendix 4.

This section has provided you with information about using three different types of surveys. Table 6 provides a quick overview of the strengths, weaknesses and uses of each of these survey styles.

	Open-Ended	**Forced Choice**	**Scaled**
Table 6. **Comparison of Different Survey Question Types**			
Use	Gather opinions on a topic	Identify common responses	Identify attitudes and beliefs
Strengths	Yields much narrative data	Easy to complete	Easiest to analyze
Weaknesses	Difficult and time-consuming to analyze	Response options may be limited	Difficult to construct questions

Distributing and Collecting Responses

After you put your survey together, you need to determine wheth-er it will be distributed in an electronic or paper format. Electronic surveys can be submitted via email to be printed and returned or as a fillable form to be completed and submitted. Electronic sur-veys come in handy if you are surveying a group where you have easy access to email addresses. You can also use a web-based col-lection method such as Survey Monkey™, or an in-house product.

The real advantage of electronic surveys is that the responses are auto-matically entered into a database, increasing the accuracy of the data since you avoid the data entry process. It also saves time later on.

Tip 7. *Check with your IT department to see what capabilities your organization has to design, collect and manage survey data.*

Of course, there is still a place for pencil-paper surveys. As the name implies, these surveys are printed out and distributed to a group. The advantage is that you receive the completed surveys all at the same time, ensuring a potentially high response rate[4]. The trade-off is that you will have to enter the data later on. Survey validity (accuracy) is another consideration. Because all your respondents are completing the survey at the same time, you have some control over social and cultural events that could affect responses. An example would be a highly publicized business acquisition or a nationally-reported school shooting. With a pencil-paper survey, you could decide to delay the implementation whereas with an on-line survey, you have no idea when or where your respondents are completing their survey. The method you choose will depend on your audience, your time-line and your available resources.

Focus Groups

The focus group is a structured interview technique which asks specific questions of a small group. The audience may either be selected for their expertise in a particular area or randomly. In our scenario, there might be two focus groups consisting of two staff members from each employment category. The group would address one of the evaluation areas of interest.

Tip 8. *In addition to gathering information about the organization, focus group results can help you design surveys. So, focus groups are sometime conducted early in the evaluation process.*

Interviews

An interview is a set of focused questions asked of specific individuals. Again the purpose is to answer one or more of the evaluation questions. Good focus group and interview questions should be specific, address the evaluation purposes and be asked the same way of all respondents. Those you interview should include key stakeholders[5] in your organization.

Observations

An observation is a structured process for collecting information about a process or activity. There are two types of observations: obtrusive and unobtrusive.

Obtrusive observations are activities where the evaluator is obviously and openly involved in an activity as an invited guest. He or she may or may not participate in the proceedings, depending on the nature of the activity.

Unobtrusive observations are those activities where the evaluator does not make his or her presence known. Observing employee interactions in the cafeteria or attending a meeting unannounced would be examples of unobtrusive observations. Both types of observations can provide information for the evaluation so long as the observations are planned, follow the established protocol, and address a specific evaluation question.

Document Reviews

Most organizations generate a trail of evidence, whether intended or not. These hard copy and electronic artifacts can provide you with valuable evaluation data. This information provides a snapshot of what the organization deems important and can provide clues about how things actually work. Oftentimes, it is just as important to look for what is NOT there as well as what is.

Examples of documents to review include websites, newsletters, publications and financial reports.

Remember that small, emergency evaluation you had to attend to earlier? The one involving the problem with the eBooks? The data you found there to solve that particular problem becomes part of your document analysis of the overall evaluation. So the time and energy you spent resolving that earlier problem feeds into the overall project.

Summary of Data Sources

In this section, we have learned about common data sources that will answer your evaluation questions. These include:

- Scaled Surveys
- Forced Choice Surveys
- Open-ended Surveys
- Focus Groups
- Individual Interviews
- Obtrusive Observations
- Unobtrusive Observations
- Document Reviews

Tip 9. *Note that all evaluation projects do not have to be broad. You may want to find out about something much smaller in scope, such as how to improve an employee orientation. The skills you are learning here can be easily applied to these smaller projects.*

Let's now revisit our evaluation questions and see how we might use these different data sources to answer them. Since this is a big project, we decided earlier that we would address all three types of evaluations, asking questions about justification, improvement and future needs.

Justification: How well has the merger gone?

1. How does the current shipment process compare to the pre-merger system?

2. How satisfied are customers with the new system?

3. How satisfied are staff and managers with the new system?

Needs Assessment: Are there new projects or products that could or should be developed?

1. What new products have you identified via web searches, attending professional conferences, or reading journals?

2. What have customers requested?

3. Are there any barriers to making these changes?

Improvement: Are there changes that can or should be made to the current system?

1. What do staff and managers suggest to improve existing products, service or processes?

2. What suggestions do customers have to improve existing products, service or processes?

3. How might the current shipment system be improved?

The next step in the plan is to identify the data sources you will need to answer these questions.

Evaluation Questions and Data Sources

To answer the **justification** questions, you would want to:

1. Gather and review the following documents:

    - Shipment turnaround times, pre- and post- merger
    - Existing customer satisfaction data (including vendors)
    - Electronic publishing data
    - Website traffic and content
    - Meeting minutes
    - Previous staff surveys

2. Interview the managers.

3. Conduct focus groups of current staff.

4. Survey customers if you do not have enough information from existing materials.

To answer the **improvement** questions, you would want to:

1. Gather and review customer complaint files and repair/return records.

2. Observe the order processing/shipment process.

3. Interview the managers.

4. Conduct focus groups of current staff

5. Scan the Internet for new products and trends.

To answer the **planning/future needs** questions, you would want to:

1. Gather and review customer complaint files and repair/return records.

2. Interview the managers.

3. Conduct focus groups of current staff.

4. Survey customers.

5. Scan the Internet for new products and trends.

At this point, you need to identify the tools you will need for the evaluation. For the observations and document reviews, you will need a checklist. For the interviews and focus groups, you will need lists of questions. For the surveys, you will need to develop the questions and collection method. You should also try to test the survey on a smaller group before you launch it to work any problems.

All of this may sound daunting, but remember that spread sheet? If you carefully track the information that you need, you can make each activity serve multiple purposes and streamline the process.

Let's use manager interviews as an example.

Note that interviewing the managers addresses all three types of evaluations and five of the questions. This means you need to make sure you ask all of these questions when you interview your managers and carefully record the responses. That way, you make good use of time and won't have to schedule a second meeting to gather additional data later. How this manager interview relates to the evaluation plan is summarized for you in Table 7.

Table 7. Manager Interview Activities	
Evaluation Type	**Evaluation Question**
Justification	*How satisfied are managers with the new system?*
Improvement	*What do managers suggest to improve existing products, service or processes?*
Improvement	*How might the current shipment system be improved?*
Planning	*What new products are on the horizon?*
Planning	*What barriers exist to making changes?*

You would engage in a similar process for each of the other data collection methods, increasing the efficiency and speed of the data collection process.

Having your evaluation plan organized in this fashion allows you to see immediately whether you are addressing your evaluation questions. If you notice any gaps, you can easily adjust your plan.

Tip 10. *As you go through the data collection process, only collect the data that will directly answer your evaluation questions. Time is of the essence!*

Once you have collected all of your data, the next step is to figure out how to analyze what you have found.

Analyzing the Data

Data analysis is the way you handle the information you have collected so that you can report the results to your audience. For quantitative data such as surveys, you may be able to do tests of statistical significance. For quantitative data, you can organize the results using content analysis.

Here are some helpful tips to help you as you work with your data:

1. Spend some time reviewing your data once it is collected.

2. Summarize each individual data source first.

3. Have someone else review your work for accuracy for both qualitative and quantitative data.

4. Make sure every data source addresses at least one of your evaluation questions.

5. Look for themes in what you are seeing.

Go back to collect more data if you have not adequately addressed one of your questions or if you are finding contradictory results. For example, if data from the staff survey contradicts what you found in the manager interview, you will need to probe deeper to get consensus. You can't just ignore contradictions; findings are findings. You just have to keep probing until you can reconcile the data.

Surveys

How you analyze survey data depends on the type of survey and how you collected the data. If your surveys are pencil-paper, someone will first have to enter the responses into a format that can be analyzed, most likely an Excel spread sheet or Access database. If you used a web-based data collection method (either in-house or something like Survey Monkey™) you should have easy access to the responses; you will just need to download it into your spreadsheet.

In either case, you will have to manipulate the data in some way before you can use it or present it to others. For dichotomous items (e.g., yes/no questions), you can only report the number and percentage of each response.

The gender question is a good example of dichotomous data.

What is your gender?		
❏ Male	❏ Female	❏ I prefer not to say

Let's say you had a total of 30 responses with 20 male and 10 female. You would indicate both the numbers and percentages in your report:

"There were a total of 30 responses to the survey. Twenty (67%) were male and 10 (33%) were female."

If you prefer, you could report the results as in Table 8.

Scaled responses give you more options for reporting results. You can report frequency distributions (number and percentage responses for each item) or measures of central tendency (usually means).

Table 8. Gender Survey Response		
	Number	Percentage
Male	20	67%
Female	10	33%
Total	30	100%

Tip 11. *Report mean scores and standard deviations only when you have a sufficiently large number of responses and when you have more than three response options.*

Because you have a large enough response and have more than three response options to your merger question, you can calculate and report mean scores and standard deviations.

Table 9 reports the mean scores, standard deviations and number of responses for the transition question.

The results of t-tests[6] shows that there were statistically significant differences in the difficulties respondents had in dealing with the Billing, HR and Customer Service departments, so these are definitely areas to explore further.

The mean score is the arithmetic average of all the responses. The standard deviation tells you how widely distributed the scores are from the mean. In this case, the higher the mean the less difficulty your respondents had with that area. This indicates that a higher score is more desirable. Conversely, higher standard deviation scores are not as desirable since that suggests less agreement among the respondents.

While Excel can calculate your mean and standard deviation scores, you will want to run statistical tests to see if your results are significant and not due to random chance. The easiest way to do this is to either export your data into a statistical package like SPSS™ or SAS™ or use an on-line statistical calculator like GraphPad.com.

"We are interested in how the merger has affected you. Please rate the difficulty the merger has been in each of the following areas:

Table 9.
Summary of Merger Affect by Area
Sorted by mean scores

	Mean	Standard Deviation	Total	Skipped Items
Billing	2.27*	0.98	30	0
HR	3.20*	1.22	30	0
Customer Service	3.38*	1.57	28	2
Data Entry	3.38	1.38	27	3
Web Support	3.39	1.72	29	1
Management	3.47	1.45	30	0
IT Support	4.03	0.68	29	1

Response Options: 1=Very difficult; 2=Difficult; 3=No affect; 4=Easy; 5=Very Easy; 0=No opinion

*Statistically significant difference between IT and Billing scores. ($p < 0.001$)

*Statistically significant difference between IT and HR scores. ($p=0.002$)

*Statistically significant difference between IT and Customer Service. ($p=0.05$)

In this example, some respondents did not answer every question, but that is OK. Simply indicate the number who did not respond and exclude those responses from your calculations. This may actually require you to re-code the data before you do the analysis.

Content Analysis

This evaluation will require that we collect quite a bit of qualitative data in the form of focus groups, interviews, observations and document review. A mistake that those who gather qualitative data often make is to do no analysis. While it is true you cannot do tests of significance as you can with survey data, you can and should organize and categorize the results. This is where content analysis comes in.

Content analysis is a systematic method of organizing and categorizing comments, observations and documents. You may purchase a software package like NVivo™ or Ethno™ or you can do the analysis yourself using a spreadsheet or database. Either approach will require that you first have a complete, verbatim transcript for interviews or focus groups and the checklist for document reviews. You then enter that information into the software package or copy to your spreadsheet. For the interview and focus group data, you would deconstruct each comment into individual units and assign each unit a category. This process takes time because even the simplest of comments can usually be broken down into several different categories. You then sort the codes and look for themes as you go.

I created an imaginary manager response to the question: *"How might the current shipping system be improved?"* as an example:

> *"We are having difficulty with meeting the time-line we have stated on the website. We are consistently running two days late. When I asked what the problem was, the order taker said she was entering it into the database right when she got the call. I looked at the database and there seems to be a lag time in updates getting posted. I think we should look into that. It could be incompatibility between the systems."*

Table 10 gives an example of what this would look like when you categorize the comments.

Table 10.
Sample Content Analysis of Interview Transcript

Category	Quote
Timeline	*We are having difficulty with meeting the timeline we have stated on the website.*
Timeline	*We are consistently running two days late.*
Database	*The order taker said she was entering it into the database right when she got the call.*
Database	*There seems to be a lag time in updates getting posted.*
Database	*It could be incompatibility between the systems.*

Note that I started with the direct quote from the interview transcript and later separated out the elements of the comments into individual units. I then assigned a category to each comment. This can be a tedious process and you will probably notice that the categories may shift a bit as you get more involved with more data, and that is OK. Having someone else review your work will help ensure that the categories you select make sense, are not biased, are valid, and are consistent.

You would use a similar process for each type of data that you are collecting. When you are finished, create an aggregated report for each group of interviews, focus groups, observations and document reviews. Spend some time mulling it over and ask one or two others to review it as well. Look for themes and questions, which you will include in your final report. Make sure that all of the comments are anonymous.

Reporting the Results

"*One of the great mistakes is to judge policies and programs by their intentions rather than their results.*"**
—Milton Friedman

The only reason to go to all the trouble of conducting an evaluation is for the results to be used to improve, justify or further develop your program. The way to do that is by presenting your findings in a way that is easy to be understood.

Here are some general tips for creating reports:

1. Use the evaluation questions to organize the report.

2. Incorporate results from all of the data sources you used.

3. Note any discrepancies or contradictions. These might need further review or may form the basis for recommendations.

4. Create more detailed and tailored reports for specific audiences.

5. Include recommendations in your report.

See Appendix 3 for a report summary template you can use to create your own reports.

In addition to a complete report of the entire evaluation, it is also helpful to have a shorter executive summary with just the highlights. For the summary, you would include the title, a short introduction, brief statement about how you implemented the evaluation, bullet points of key findings, conclusions and your recommendations.

Part 3.

Beyond the Basics

> **"It's not what you look at that matters,
> it's what you see."**
>
> **—Henry David Thoreau**

So far, you have learned how to plan and implement a program evaluation using traditionally accepted methods and approaches. Following this process will *usually* allow you to achieve the goal of answering your evaluation questions.

However, there are times when you will have to do more. Either your questions are too complex or the type of information you need is very high stakes. For whatever, reason, you may need to do more so it is always good to have additional methods at your disposal.

This section give you three more evaluative tools you can use to collect, understand and organize your data: the *Delphi Technique, Critical Incident Method* and *Root Cause Analysis.*

We will first look at the Delphi Technique.

The Delphi Technique

In ancient Greece, those seeking answers to the questions of the day could visit the famous Oracle of Delphi. There the priestesses of Apollo would receive esteemed visitors from all over the world. They would entertain their questions and respond, usually in cryptic fashion. Today we still need answers but we don't need to travel to ancient Greece. We can consult our own experts using the Delphi Technique.

If you are not sure about the best way to approach a problem or need professional advice, a Delphi approach might be helpful. This structured group interview process is designed to seek consensus among a group of experts about a question, concept or process and has a fairly defined process:

1. Identify the experts. (7-12 is a good number.)

2. Develop and send a few initial open-ended questions to your experts. Or, alternatively, you can convene your group either face-to-face or real-time video chat. Refer back to page 25 for information on constructing open-ended questions.

3. Clarify the responses you are getting then develop a questionnaire based on your information and send that out to your group. Your survey can either be pencil-paper or electronic. See page 23 for information on surveys.

4. Your panel then responds to the questionnaire. You tabulate the results and send them the list. You then ask them to rate or rank the issues that have been developed.

5. When you get the responses back, you should have a consensus answer to your question. You tabulate the results of the final round and share the answer with your experts and incorporate that piece of data into your evaluation report.

Even though this is qualitative data, the results carry weight because it is based on expert opinion.

In our scenario, a process like this might be useful if you find a lack of consensus or cannot answer a specific question. Your experts would include staff from **all levels** of the company from the CEO on down. After identifying your group, you would send out an email describing the process along with a few well con-structed open-ended questions designed to get answers to specific questions. You would analyze the results using content analysis techniques described earlier and report results back to your expert panel. Because your expert panel would probably include manag-ers and staff, you might get more honest feedback if you gather the data using an anonymous electronic source like Survey Monkey (TM)rather than email.

Critical Incident Method

While interviewing the experts may help you identify ways to address a specific issue, using the Critical Incident Method can be helpful if you need to clarify tasks associated with a particular activity. Jonassen, Hannum, and Tessmer (1989) define critical incidents as "reports of observed behavior that are recorded then analyzed to determine various performance dimensions of a task." (p. 245) The process includes the following:

1. Collect the incidents via document review and reports.

2. Identify the specific behaviors associated with the incidents.

3. Identify how they relate to specific tasks and their
   relative importance.

By collecting and analyzing incident reports, you might be able to more clearly clarify job duties. This might be useful in a case like our scenario where there has been a merger and roles might be blurred or need to be reconfigured. What you learn may very well become the basis of a subsequent program improvement project.

Root Cause Analysis

Where the Critical Incident Method focuses on specific tasks, Root Cause Analysis takes a broader systems approach. This evaluative tool is widely used in the medical community to review unusual incidents and arrive at possible solutions. The purpose is to identify the reason (root cause) of a problem and seek ways to prevent the problem from happening again. Root Cause Analysis focuses on systems issues and starts with the premise that problems that occur are multi-faceted in nature and not the result of individual error. Root Cause Analysis seeks to shift from "shaming and blaming" of a specific individual to looking at the process as a whole. The Agency for Healthcare Research and Quality (http://www.psnet.ahrq.gov/primer.aspx?primerID=10) is the best source of information on the Root Cause Analysis methodology.

Let's go back to the imaginary narrative comments from the manager about problems with shipping and see how a Root Cause Analysis might inform our evaluation.

> *"We are having difficulty with meeting the time-line we have stated on the website. We are consistently running two days late. When I asked what the problem was, the order taker said she was entering it into the database right when she got the call. I looked at the database and there seems to be a lag time in updates getting posted. I think we should look into that. It could be incompatibility between the systems."*

Some variation of a Root Cause Analysis might be the perfect way to address this problem and provide additional data for your evaluation. This situation obviously is not any one person's fault and involves multiple players. It is a systems issue. Gathering everyone involved for an honest discussion of the problem may result in a great solution that no one individually could have imagined by themselves.

For a Root Cause Analysis to truly work, several conditions must exist:

1. The process needs to be clearly spelled out.

2. There needs to be an experienced convener. [8]

3. Everyone involved must feel free to speak openly.

4. There must be no fear of reprisal.

5. Results need to be reported and shared.

6. Solutions need to be implemented and tested.

Reports that come out of your analysis, as with data from the Delphi Technique and critical Incident become additional sources of information about your program.

Final thoughts

This guide has hopefully provided you with a concise overview of the evaluation process. Perhaps you are now more confident in your ability to plan your evaluation and understand that a good evaluation, large or small, can be a manager's best friend.

By following the guidelines of developing your questions, collecting appropriate data, and reporting results, you will gain valuable information that can help you improve an existing activity, determine whether you have met your goals and/or plan new programs.

End Notes

[1] Groteleuschen A (1980). "Program evaluation", in Knox, A. (Ed). *Developing, administering and evaluating adult education.* San Francisco: Jossey-Bass.

[2] Two ways to overcome potential bias are, first, to be aware that bias is a possibility and, second, to work with others throughout the process. If you want to read more about ways to avoid bias, I refer you to Alan Peshkin's appendix, "The subjective I" in *The color of strangers the color of friends.*

[3] Generalizability can be defined as the degree to which findings from one situation can be applied in other settings. This is a desired outcome for research but not necessarily for evaluation.

[4] Response rate is defined as the number and percentage of people who complete and return your survey.

[5] Stakeholders are those who are highly invested in the outcomes of the project or activity. These can include those inside and outside the organization.

[6] T-tests look for the differences between two groups and generate p-values. P-values are used to determine if there is a significant difference between two mean scores. P-values that are less than 0.05 are generally considered to be statistically significant.

[7] Jonassen, Hannum, and Tessmer, p. 395.

[8] Root Cause Analysis conveners might benefit from special training in communication and group dynamics.

Appendices

1. Kirkpatrick's Levels of Learning Model

Donald Kirkpatrick provides a very good way to evaluate individual performance. He identified four levels of evaluation which are:

1 - **Reaction:** Measures how satisfied participants were with the training.

2 - **Learning:** Measures what participants have learned from the training.

3 - **Behavior:** Measures whether what was learned is being applied on the job.

4 - **Results:** Measures whether the application of training is achieving results.

Reaction and learning can be considered necessary but not sufficient for assessing learning. Good evaluations of employee learning should look for changes in behavior with the ideal to be able to measure actual results.

Kirkpatrick, D (1998). *Evaluating training programs: The four levels*. San Francisco: Berrett-Koehler Publications, Inc.

2. General Evaluation Planning Template

Here is an outline you can use to develop your own evaluation plan. Feel free to copy and use.

Planning (This helps you clarify the situation for yourself).

1. Briefly describe the problem.

2. Identify why it is important to resolve the problem.

3. Do a literature search to see what has been done in this area. (It can be helpful to see how others have approached this issue.)

4. Identify what you hope to accomplish by the evaluation.

5. Identify the evaluation purpose(s) (Needs Assessment, Program Improvement, Program Justification)

Evaluation Questions. Identify evaluation questions that address your evaluation purpose(s). Make sure the questions are specific and relevant to the purpose. Try to limit the number of questions.

Identify ways you will collect the information:

1. Observations (direct and/or indirect)

2. Interviews (staff, managers, clients, other)

3. Focus groups (staff, managers, clients, other)

4. Surveys (staff, managers, clients, other)

5. Document review (company logs, records, meeting minutes, publications, web pages, etc.)

6. Pre- and post- testing

Identify data collection methods you might have to develop:

1. Observation sheet

2. Interview questions

3. Focus group questions

4. Survey questions (Use previous surveys where possible for comparison purposes.)

5. Checklists for document reviews

6. Knowledge tests

3. Evaluation Report Format

Here is an outline you can use to develop your evaluation plan. Feel free to copy and adapt. See http://www.barrett-evaluations. com/forms.html for free downloadable forms.

Evaluation of the [Program]

Prepared by [Name]

Date

Introduction (Purpose and goals of the evaluation.)

Methodology (How you did the evaluation.)

1. List of evaluation questions.

2. Literature review if applicable.

3. Types of data collected. (e.g., surveys, observations, interviews, focus groups, document review)

4. Who you evaluated. (e.g., employees, managers, customers)

5. Dates of evaluation.(e.g. employee survey distributed January 15, 2013)

6. Brief description of surveys, interview questions, etc.

Findings (Organized by evaluation questions. Include tables and figures as relevant. Be sure to include sample comments to illustrate your points.)

Conclusions (Bring the findings together.)

Recommendations (Your suggestions of next steps based on the findings.)

Appendix (Include copies of questions, document review checklists and surveys.)

4. Evaluation Resources

General References

Root Cause Analysis, Agency for Healthcare Research and Quality. http://www.psnet.ahrq.gov/primer.aspx?primerID=10 Last cited 3/15/2015.

Fitzpatrick J, Sanders J, and Worthen B. (2004). *Program evaluation: alternative approaches and practical guidelines* (3rd Edition). Boston: Allyn and Bacon.

Groteleuschen A (1980). "Program evaluation" in Knox, A. (Ed). *Developing, administering and evaluating adult education.* San Francisco: Jossey-Bass.

Jonassen, D; Hannum, W. and Tessmer, W. (1989). *Handbook of task analysis procedures.* New York: Praeger.

Kirkpatrick, D (1998). *Evaluating training programs: the four levels.* San Francisco: Berrett-Koehler Publications, Inc.

Merriam S. (2009) *Qualitative research: A guide to design and implementation.* San Francisco: Jossey-Bass.

Peshkin, A. (1991). "The subjective I," in *The color of strangers the color of friends.* Chicago: University of Chicago Press.

Stufflebeam D and Shinkfield A. (2007) *Evaluation theory, models, and applications.* San Francisco: Jossey-Bass.

Logic Model References

Logic Model Template http://img.docstoccdn.com/thumb/orig/545308.png

National Network of Libraries of Medicine *Guide 5: Define how a program will work - The logic model* (http://nnlm.gov/outreach/community/logicmodel.html)

Sample logic model (https://encrypted-tbn1.gstatic.com/images?q=tbn:ANd9GcT0Vx4D8CGOB5h7zQ4b6DtuSFHd7mF-gU8B0FYevufgqauOmw5S3)

University of Wisconsin Extension Logic Model Templates http://www.uwex.edu/ces/pdande/evaluation/evallogicmodelworksheets.html

Survey Research References

General survey research http://www.socialresearchmethods.net/kb/survey.php

http://gsociology.icaap.org/methods/surveys.htm

Survey Research Lab, University of Illinois-Chicago http://www.srl.uic.edu/srllink/srllink.htm

University of Connecticut (Likert scales) http://researchbasics.education.uconn.edu/likert_scales/

Sunnycrest Press

Sunnycrest Press

Sunnycrest Press is a specialized publisher located in Springfield, Illinois. Email office@sunnycrestpress.com if you have questions or want more information.

Who we are:

Jerry Barrett, President. 25 years' experience in graphic and web design with special interest in cartoons. He has expertise in the printing industry.

Nancy Barrett, Director of Operations. 25 years' experience in program development with expertise in budgeting and project management. She is currently the Coordinator of Assessment and Accreditation with the College of Education and Human Services at the University of Illinois Springfield.

Made in the USA
San Bernardino, CA
19 August 2018